It's Fun to Learn About Feelings

An Emotional Intelligence Curriculum for Children (Grades 2 - 5)

Including Fun Games, Activites and Reproducible Worksheets

That Help Children Explore and Express Emotions from the Inside Out

youth light
inc.

© 2008 by YouthLight, Inc.
Chapin, SC 29036

Cover Design and Layout by GraphicSolutions, Inc.
Project Editing by Susan Bowman

ISBN
978-1-59850-061-5

Library of Congress Number
2008939026

10 9 8 7 6 5 4 3
Printed in the United States

Table of contents

About The Authors

Carol Wood was born in the UK. She studied Counseling and Child Psychology at the University of Queensland, Australia and has been working as an Educational Psychologist for 20 years, helping Children and Families. Carol is also a self-taught artist.

She felt inspired to develop a program for children that would help them express their feelings using fun and creativity as she felt this was a major key in helping them to feel good about themselves and thus gain a healthier sense of self worth.

She felt that this type of program would help children to express outwardly what's happening for them on the inside. It would help them to clear emotional hurts from their body and also help them to develop more effective communication skills.

Carol has combined her skills in Teaching, Counseling and Art to develop the Rainbow Planet Connection Programs and Resources.

Karyn Nash, from Australia, has been a Primary School Teacher for 20 years. She has worked extensively with children with learning difficulties.

She is passionate about helping children to be healthy well-balanced individuals and to feel good about themselves. She is currently using the resources to assist children to change their energy state to a more peaceful one and also to learn how express themselves without hurting or blaming others. She has had some wonderful results.

Karyn has brought her Computer and Graphic Design skills into this project and has contributed greatly to the wonderful, visually attractive resources that are available from the Rainbow Planet Connection.

Note to Parents, Teachers and Other Caregivers
WHAT DO YOU WANT FOR YOUR CHILDREN?

• Do you want to raise your children to be emotionally and physically healthy, to be good communicators and to have good sense of self-worth?

• Do you want to encourage them to develop and express their own unique talents and abilities and lead a happy, fulfilling life?

The reality (or illusion) is that they often come across challenging situations as they experience life. These may include bullying, friendship issues, changes and loss. These situations bring certain emotions into play such as anger, anxiety and sadness. You may not be able to protect them from encountering these situations, but you can support them in processing and releasing these emotions.

There is a growing awareness in our society of children's social and emotional needs. Many children can become damaged adults if they do not deal with their emotional hurts.

While we want to encourage children to process and release those emotional hurts which may be affecting their self-worth, we also want them to increase the presence of more loving feelings which will help them to feel happier and more content inside.

We would like to support you, as parents, teachers and other caregivers, in growing socially and emotionally happy, healthy children.

Carol and Karyn

Helping Children Understand and Express Feelings

This book has been have been developed to assist children and parents to understand and become more aware of their feelings and how they are affecting others around them and themselves. It offers children ways of exploring and processing emotional hurts in a fun, creative way, using Art, Drama, Dance, Movement, Story-Telling, Journal Writing and other self-expression activities.

This book can be used by parents, teachers, child-care workers, counselors and others to help children with their social/emotional development.

A proactive approach is offered, which can help children to develop skills and techniques that can be used to process and release feelings. Strategies for children include: deep breathing to change the energy state; breathing out feelings; doing physical activity such as dance to release pent up emotional energy; using art to express inner feelings; using drama/role play to help them to express and understand their own and other people's feelings; using story-telling and journal writing to process and express their feelings.

Inner Emotional State

This includes helping children to:

- Develop an awareness of breathing and how this affects their emotional state.

- Understand how their body responds to outside experiences and influences and how this affects breathing and body tension.

- Recognize the body signals when they have tension and turmoil happening inside.

- Use Visualization/Relaxation exercises to develop a sense of inner awareness and to change their emotional state to a more peaceful one.

- Develop a stronger sense of self-worth and self-acceptance.

Outward Expression

This book helps children to understand that feelings are okay and are part of the way we express ourselves. The activities and techniques in this book help children EXPRESS OUTWARDLY WHAT'S HAPPENING ON THE INSIDE, using Art, Drama, Dance/Movement, Story-Telling and Journal Writing.

This includes helping children to:

• Be responsible for their own feelings and emotional state.

• Be responsible for the behavioral choices they make as a result of how they are feeling and thinking.

• Use creative self-expression to help release and express these emotions, allowing them to flow so that it is no longer stuck in the body causing stress and turmoil.

• Use physical release through movement and physical activity to assist in releasing the energy of pent up emotions.

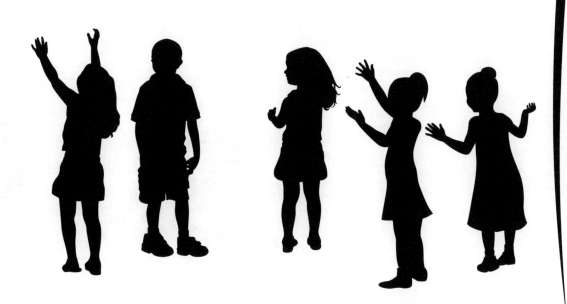

Introduction

This book provides stimulus materials to assist children, teenagers and adults to explore and express their feelings, using fun games and activities.

A black and white set of Feeling Cards is included with this book. These are also available in color and sold separately through YouthLight. Most of the activities in this book can be used by children in the second through fifth grade.

The cards and the activities can be used by teachers, counselors, childcare workers, people who run workshops or therapy groups and most importantly by parents, who can use them with their children.

These activities can be used in a classroom, with small groups or individual children.

"I've used the Feelings Cards in groups with young people and parents. The biggest surprise was when I had them in a middle of a group of men. Each man picked a card and introduced themselves to the others, talking through the card about their feelings. They said the cards were great as they assisted them in connecting with emotions that are not always easy to identify. I recommend these cards for teachers, counselors, people who run workshops and importantly for families to use on a daily basis."

Testimonial from Amrita Hobbs
Author of "Getting Real" Books and Workshops
www.amritahobbs.com

Why Explore and Express Emotions?

Many of us externalize and express our unresolved feelings of anger, sadness, anxiety and fear with negative and sometimes antisocial behaviors and actions, which can be harmful to ourselves and others.

Some of us choose to suppress our feelings, but this may affect us in the long term with diseases of the mind and body. It may manifest at later stages as depression, anxiety, defiant behavior or other mental or physical illnesses.

It's important to acknowledge that feelings and emotions are okay; they are part of the way we learn about ourselves and others. We can encourage the exploration and expression of these emotions in fun, creative ways without hurting or blaming others.

Studies show that children are more likely to lead successful, emotionally well-balance lives, if they are considerate of other people's feelings, from an early age.

Dr. Claude Steiner states in his book, "Emotional Literacy; Intelligence with a Heart" (Steiner, 2000), "To be emotionally literate is to be able to handle emotions in a way that improves your personal power and improves the quality of life for you and equally important the quality of life for the people around you. Emotional literacy helps your emotions to work for you instead of against you. It improves relationships, creates loving possibilities between people, makes cooperative work possible, and facilitates the feeling of community."

From http://www.claudesteiner.com

The Model offered on the following page, provides a visual way of showing the possible outcomes if we express our feelings with blame and try to dump them on others or if we choose healthier ways of expressing how we feel. It also shows the possible outcomes of suppressing emotions.

Depending on which path we choose, we can be powerful and responsible for our own thoughts, feelings and behaviors and what we create in our lives, or we can choose to be powerless victims and blame others or the world in general.

It is of benefit, to help children be aware of and to process and release lower fear-based emotions such as anger, anxiety and shame. This will help to prevent disease and depression. These fear-based emotions can increase the production of adrenalin in our bodies and lead to suppression of the immune system and disease.

We can also encourage children to increase the presence of love-based emotions such as joy, appreciation, and enthusiasm. These love-based, emotions increase the production of endorphins in our bodies, providing us with a sense of well-being and contentment.

Emotional Suppression or Expression Model

Our world - Our perceptions of situations and experiences filtered through our senses	

↓

Thoughts created by the mind in response to external events

↓

Emotions come up – emotions are okay they provide us with a way of checking our reaction to external events (How we process them is them is important.)

↓

Point of Awareness and Choice "I'm feeling angry. What am I going to do with this feeling? Am I going to be a victim? Who does this feeling belong to?"

↙ ↘

SUPRESS EMOTIONS	EXPRESS EMOTIONS	
↓	↙	↘
Often we lock emotions inside. We suppress them (maybe for years). They may come out later.	We can find other ways to process and express emotions without blaming or hurting others. Be responsible. BE POWERFUL.	We can dump emotions on others using Blame and Rendering us POWERLESS.
↓	↓	↓
Dysfunctional Behavior	Use creative outlets like Art, Journal Writing, Music, Dance, Physical Exercise, talk it over, communicate without blame	Feel okay?
↓		↙ ↘
Can lead to Disease of body and mind such as depression, inner suppression of anger, anxiety etc. Build up of an emotional pain in body.		YES	NO
↓	↓	↓	↓
Feeling like a victim POWERLESS Hanging on to fear - based emotions. Guilt, shame, blame.	Creates positive self-talk and belief systems. RAISE SELF-WORTH.	Temporary feeling of Control and Power	Guilt or other Unpleasant emotions
↓		↓	↓
Creates negative self-talk and belief systems. Contributes to LOWER SELF-WORTH.		Creates negative self-talk and belief systems. Contributes to LOWER SELF-WORTH.	

Benefits Of Using The Feeling Cards

The games and activities in this book promote the development of Social and Emotional Literacy skills by helping children to:

- Manage and be responsible for their own feelings.

- Explore and express their feelings without blaming others.

- Become more aware of how body language and facial expressions can be used to interpret feelings.

- Be aware of their emotional triggers when interacting with others.

- Be more aware of how others may be feeling and to make choices about their emotional responses to others.

How to Use

The fun activities and games in this book can be used by teachers wishing to develop a more proactive approach to dealing with challenging situations that can often arise in the classroom, including friendship issues, bullying, 'put-downs' and teasing.

Many of the activities also support the development of more effective communication and social skills in children. They can be used to teach children more effective skills in these areas.

These activities can easily be incorporated into a classroom management program, to assist in the creation of a co-operative and harmonious environment.

The activities have been divided into five sections, as described in the table of contents. This allows you to easily locate an appropriate activity to suit your needs.

Many of the activities can be used on a repeat basis and become part of your weekly program to enhance healthy social and emotional development in the children.

Useful Tips

Encouraging children to be responsible for as well as to explore and express their feelings is a major theme which is used throughout the book.

Many children have a tendency to play the victim role and to try to blame others for their feelings. It is important to you as a facilitator to be persistent in encouraging them to take responsibility for their own feelings and responses.

You can hand the responsibility back to them by asking questions such as:

• How do you feel when...?

• What can you do to express that feeling? (without hurting or blaming others)

• What might happen if you respond that way?

Questions are used extensively throughout these activities to help children to understand, explore and express their emotions in ways that are beneficial and supportive of themselves and others.

It will greatly improve the outcomes for the children, if you as a facilitator participate in the activities and use the techniques offered in this book.

The children are learning valuable skills, which will benefit them for life, when they take responsibility for their feelings and communicate them to others in appropriate non-violent ways.

{Section One}

My Feelings

Activity 1
Guess the Feeling

Objective: To help children be more aware of how they and others may be feeling, using clues such as body language, movement and facial expression.

Note: This activity can be used as a warm up, fun activity.

What you need

- Feelings Cards on pages 85-92 (If using this activity with younger children you may need to select some of the easier feeling words such as Happy, Sad and Angry.)

What to do

- Ask one of the children in the group (or the individual child if using one on one), to choose a card at random from the Feelings Cards set, without looking at it or showing it to anyone else. Ask them to hold the card so that the other children can't see it.

- Ask the child to look at the card and mime out the feeling on the card, using facial expression, body language and movement. Younger children may need assistance from the facilitator.

- Ask the others in the group to guess the feeling that is being mimed. If no one can guess the feeling then sound and voice can be used to help to identify the feeling.

- The child who guesses correctly has the next turn.

Discussion

Using the cards that have been selected or others, if appropriate, discuss how we can pick up clues about how someone is feeling, even if they are not speaking. We can pick up these clues by observing their body language, movement and facial expression.

The following questions can be used for prompts if necessary.
- How can we tell how someone is feeling, even when he or she doesn't speak?
- How can we tell when someone is feeling Happy? Sad? Angry? Discuss other feelings if appropriate.

Note: This activity can be followed by Activity 2 and 8, which help children to look at their responses to other people's feelings.

Extension Idea

Further discussion can be generated on how we can tell how someone is feeling by their tone of voice, words and language.

Optional Activity

Worksheet: Guess the Feeling — Ask the children to write or draw their understanding of body language, facial expressions and tone of voice and language of the various emotions.

Guess the Feeling

Draw pictures or write descriptions about the Facial Expressions, Body Language and Posture, Tone of Voice and Words of each of the feelings.

	Facial Expression	Body Language & Posture	Tone of Voice/ Words/Language
Angry			
Excited			
Sad			
Happy			

Activity 2
When have you felt like this?

Objectives: To help children to be more aware of how different feelings are brought to the surface as a result of external situations and/or interactions with others.
To be aware of possible emotional responses to various situations.

What you need
• Feelings Cards (If using this activity with younger children you may need to select some of the easier feeling words such as Happy, Sad and Angry.)

What to do
• Place the cards from the Feelings Cards pack face down on the table or floor in the middle of the group. Ask the children to take turns picking a card at random from the middle.

• When one child has picked a card, ask them to read it out and then ask the group the following questions:
  • When in your life do you or have you felt like this?
  • How do you know when you are feeling like this? What does your body tell you? What do your thoughts tell you?
    Possible answers: pain in heart, feel rejected, think I'm no good.
  • What situations cause you to feel like this?
    Possible answers: When someone shouts at me, teases me, when I feel left out.

- How do you know when others are feeling like this? What does their body tell you? What do their actions tell you?
  Possible answers: I can tell by their tone of voice, facial expression.
- Focus on one feeling at a time.
- These questions can be written on the board as a Chart and filled in according to the children's responses.

Please Note

As a facilitator, encourage the children to find ways of expressing their unpleasant feelings without taking them out on other people.

Note: This activity can be followed by Activity 8, which helps children to look at their responses to other people's feelings.

Optional Activity

Worksheet: When Have You Felt Like This? (on the following page) — Ask the children to choose one feeling and complete the questions on their activity sheet. You may like to do multiple copies so children can explore a variety of feelings.

When Have You Felt Like This?

Write the name of a feeling in the centre box. Answer the questions in the surrounding circles.

When in your life do you or have you felt like this?

How do you know when others are feeling like this? What does their body tell you? What do their actions tell you?

Feeling Word

How do you know when you are feeling like this? What does your body tell you? What do your thoughts tell you?

What situations cause you to feel like this?

Activity 3
Cards in the corner

Objective: To help children express and release feelings from their body so that they are fully present in the classroom and ready to focus on learning.

What you need

• Feelings Cards

Preparation

• Before the children come into the classroom have a number of selected feelings cards placed at various points around the room.

What to do

• When they come in, ask them to go and stand by the card that best describes how they are feeling today.

• Children can then be encouraged to share the reason they are feeling that way. Have a 'Show and Tell' session.

• You may need to limit the amount of time allocated for each child.

Note: Further support may be needed for some children with more extreme emotional issues.

Extension Idea

Note: This is an exercise in listening and acknowledging the children's feelings. If you think it would help the children to process their feelings then you may like to continue with the following:

- Once the child has identified a feeling e.g. ANGER, ask them, "What can you do to help yourself express that feeling so that you are not holding on to it all day? What might happen if you stay ANGRY during class today? Is it okay to take your feelings out on others around you?"

- You may like to create a *Calm Down Corner* in your classroom or home. This process is described on the following page. The children can then use the corner, when needed, to process and express their emotional energy and then return to the group when they are calmer and more receptive to learning.

Optional Activity

Create your own Feeling Card that will help you feel good today. Color and decorate your card. Place in a prominent place as a reminder to have a positive attitude throughout the day.

Take a leaf from the Palm
Keep Cool Stay Calm

Count to 10

Take a Deep Breath

Imagine a peaceful place in your mind

Write in Your Journal

Close Your Eyes

What is a 'Calm Down Corner'?

A 'Calm Down Corner' is a place in the classroom or home, which has been set-aside for Time Out. It may include Cushions, Relaxing Music or Relaxation CD's, Art Materials and Personal Journals.

What is the Purpose of this 'Calm Down Corner'?

- To encourage children to recognize when they need some personal space and to choose to go to the 'Calm Down Corner' to be on their own for a short time.

- To allow children to choose to remove themselves from situations which are uncomfortable or unpleasant for them.

- To provide children with an area where they can choose to take time out to change their emotional state. For example if a situation is becoming heated and developing into a win/lose battle, then children may choose to take time out to think about what is happening and to look at ways of expressing their emotions without blaming others.

- To allow children to relax and recharge or refocus.

- To allow children to express how they are feeling using Art or Journal Writing or other Creative Expression Activities.

You may want to create a poster for your 'Calm Down Corner', similar to "The Calm Palm,"' illustrated on the previous page. You can also use a pole or broomstick for the base and attach palm leaves using green construction paper.

It will be more effective, if you as a Parent or Teacher also use the 'Calm Down Corner' and act as a Role Model for your children.

Activity 4
How would you feel?

Objectives: To encourage discussion of feelings and reactions to situations which occur in life.
To raise awareness and encourage discussion that different options or choices can result in different possible outcomes.

What you need

• Worksheet: How Would You Feel Scenario Cards on page 30. A number of short scenarios which can be photocopied and cut and pasted onto colored cards.

• Feelings Cards (If using this activity with younger children you may need to select some of the easier feeling words such as Happy, Sad and Angry.)

Preparation

• Have a range of cards available with different situations/scenarios, which provoke a range of different reactions and feelings. You can make up some more of your own scenarios which are relevant to your particular situation, or you can ask the children to create some relevant to them, perhaps anonymously.

What to do

• Place the scenario cards upside down in the center of a table or on the floor.

• Spread the Feeling Cards out around the scenario cards, so that they can see and access these easily.

- Ask a child in the group to pick a card and read the short scenario out loud. Then ask them to read out the questions on the card one at a time. For the first question "How would you feel?", ask the child to pick a card from the Feelings Cards pack which best describes how they might feel in response to the situation described.

- Ask a few other children in the group to pick a card for the same situation. Discuss. Are they all the same or are there a range of feeling responses to the same situation?

- Continue this process using the other questions on the Scenario Cards, such as "How would you react?" and "What might you do?" Discuss if the outcome is a win/win, lose/win or lose/lose situation. If appropriate, ask "What can you do to change this to a win/win for everyone?"

- Repeat this process with the other Scenario Cards.

Note: Encourage the children to be responsible for their feelings. Explain that it's okay to have these feelings but they can learn to express them without hurting or blaming others.

Extension Idea
- Ask each child to make up a situation of their own either imaginary or real.

- Ask them to read it out to others in class. The others can ask them, "How would you feel?" "How would you react?"

Optional Activity
Role play a few scenarios, either the ones given or the ones the children have created, with different outcomes. Discuss these differences.

How would you feel?
Scenario Cards

Scenario: Your mom or dad won a free ticket to a theme park and said you were going this weekend. **Questions:** How would you feel? How would you react? What might you do?	**Scenario:** Your teacher is upset with you because you haven't done your homework. **Questions:** How would you feel? How would you react? What might you do? Is this helpful and beneficial for you? Will it solve the problem or make it worse? What are some other choices for dealing with this situation? What might be their outcomes?
Scenario: Another kid pushes you around on the playground. **Questions:** How would you feel? How would you react? What might you do? Is this helpful and beneficial for you? Will it solve the problem or make it worse? What are some other choices for dealing with this situation? What might be their outcomes?	**Scenario:** You've lost your pet dog. **Questions:** How would you feel? How would you react? What might you do?
	Scenario: Your Dad takes you somewhere special. **Questions:** How would you feel? How would you react? What might you do?
Scenario: A friend doesn't want to be your friend anymore. **Questions:** How would you feel? How would you react? What might you do? Is this helpful and beneficial for you? Will it solve the problem or make it worse? What are some other choices for dealing with this situation? What might be their outcomes?	**Scenario:** Your Mom and Dad are always arguing. **Questions:** How would you feel? How would you react? What might you do? Is this helpful and beneficial for you? Will it solve the problem or make it worse? What are some other choices for dealing with this situation? What might be their outcomes?

Activity 5
Pick the Feeling

Objectives: To encourage children to express visually and verbally how they are feeling in the present moment.

To help children understand how others may be feeling.

To help them to explore their choices and to find more beneficial responses to difficult situations.

To encourage them not to take out their unpleasant feelings on others.

Note: This activity can be used by teachers, counselors or by parents with the individual children involved when an incident has triggered off strong feelings. It is useful for conflict situations to allow each person to take time out to listen to the other person's feelings and also to express their own. It helps to depersonalize the situation. It may need to be adapted for use with younger children as a certain amount of reasoning skills are involved.

What you need
• Feelings Cards

What to do
(This activity is more effective if it is directly linked with an incident that is currently occurring in the child's life, which evokes feelings.)
• STEP ONE — Listening and acknowledging the child.
  This step is just about helping the child to understand more about their own and other people's feelings and responses.
  • Copy page 33 and ask the children to draw or describe a situation that is happening in their life now that is bringing up strong feelings and then to pick a card (or 2-3 cards) to best describe how they are feeling. For example: Ask, "How do you feel about your little brother always telling tales about you to your mom?" Pick some cards that best describe your feelings.

Stimulus questions may be needed to help a child identify and express the feeling. "What happened? What did you do? What did the other person do? How do you feel? How do you think they feel?"
(Pick cards) Ask, "Does this happen a lot?"

- STEP TWO helping the child to find a more beneficial solution.
  - Introduce the concept to the child that they have choices as to how they respond to other people. Ask them the following questions to determine if they are willing to make a commitment to change the situation. "Do you want this to keep happening? Do you want to change it? Are you willing to take responsibility for your part in this?"

  - Discuss different responses and reactions with the child with regard to the same situation. Discuss which ones might be better for everyone involved.

  - Ask them, "How would you feel if this situation was resolved?" Choose some cards that best describe how you might feel.

Extension Idea

This exercise can help to diffuse the energy and release feelings from the body.

Ask the child to focus on one unpleasant feeling that they are currently experiencing. Ask, "Would you like to let go of this feeling? Where in the body is this feeling, close your eyes and try to find it. What color is it? Lets try breathing it out." Use deep breathing techniques to help the child breathe the feeling out of the body.

Now ask, "How would you like to feel instead? What color and shape is this new feeling. Let's breathe this in to replace the other feeling." Use deep breathing techniques to help the child breathe this feeling into their body.

How do I Handle my Feelings?

Think of situations when you have unpleasant feelings. Choose 1 feeling and write or draw in the boxes below to describe the situation which brings up this feeling.

Situation – I am feeling _____ because

What happened?	What did I do or say to cause this?	What did other people do or say to cause this?

⇩

How do I know I am feeling _____? What does my body say? What does my mind say?

⇩

It's okay to have this feeling but BE RESPONSIBLE AND POWERFUL. Ask yourself, How can I express this feeling, without taking it out on or blaming others?

⇩

How can I change my attitude so I feel good again?

Activity 6
That's Life

Objectives: To help children to identify areas in life that are causing them stress or difficulty.

> To encourage them to explore and express the feelings associated with the stress or difficulty.
>
> To come up with different ways of responding to and generating possible solutions to these issues.

What you need
• Feelings Cards

What to do
• Discuss and help the child to identify the situations that may be causing problems. Come up with the most important ones — friendships, bullying, homework, family. Target one area at a time that is causing concern, e.g. How do you feel about — homework? your parent's divorce? your big brother teasing you?'

• Ask the child (teenager or adult) to tell you a little story about what's happening. It doesn't have to be very long as the cards will help the child to get in touch with feelings and hopefully open up more to sharing what's really happening. Your job here is just to listen and encourage the child to express him/herself.

- Ask child to pick one or more cards to describe how they are feeling about this specific situation. Some cards that may be picked here may be worried, lazy, scared, upset, e.g. Worried about homework being too difficult. Lazy because they can't get motivated.

- Ask him/her to tell you more about each feeling, e.g. Tell me more about your homework, are you finding it too difficult? Are you having trouble setting aside time to do it? Do you keep putting it off?'

- Together come up with possible solutions. Let the child pick which ones they feel they would like to follow up with. Using the following page have children formulate an action plan.

Feelings Action Plan

Complete the following questionnaire to explore how you are feeling about a current situation in your life and generate possible solutions.

1. What is the problem? Describe in your own words.

2. How do I feel now about this situation? Choose Feelings Cards

3. What are some possible solutions?

4. Which one/s shall I choose? Action Plan.

5. How might/will I feel when this situation is resolved? Choose Feeling Cards.

6. If the Solution you chose does not produce a positive outcome go back to Step 3 or 4 to generate and/or choose another solution.

Activity 7
Emotions Box

Objectives: To allow expression of written feelings. To generate possible choices of response and consequent outcomes to a variety of life situations.

What you need

- Feelings Cards
- Pieces of paper for writing out situations and feelings
- A colorful box

What to do

- Tell the children that they can write about situations in their life that have brought up some unpleasant feelings such as anger, sadness, fear, or pleasant feelings such as happiness, calmness and excitement.

- They can post this in the box when they have finished, anonymously.

- With class or group: Take time out to read out what the children have written. Discuss possible solutions.

- These real life situations can be used as stimulus material for role plays.

The following model can be used to explain to the children that they are responsible for the choices they make and the outcomes that result from these choices. If they don't like the outcome, they have the option of making changes at various points in the model. You may like to use one or more of the situations discussed in the previous activity as examples to help reinforce choices resulting in various outcomes. You could have the children to role play these situations.

SITUATION
(triggers)

⇩

THOUGHTS & SELF TALK
(leads to)

⇩

FEELINGS AND BELIEFS ABOUT SELF
(Determines)

⇩

REACTION & OUTCOMES
(Reinforces Beliefs about Self)

Two Possible Outcomes

The following example shows two possible outcomes for the same situation.

1. Situation: Friends don't want to play with me at the moment.

2. He/she doesn't like me.
   I'm no good. I'm not likable.

3. Sad. Depressed. Rejected.
   I can't make friends.

4. Sulk/Get angry with friend/
   Take it out on family members
   Feel more lonely and rejected.

It's his/her choice and I accept that.
I'm still okay.

I need to be confident and h appy
with myself.
I can find something else to do or
another friend to play with.

I can create your own fun and be
self-reliant.
I will make more friends and create
other fun things to do.

Extension Idea

Role-plays — You can extend this activity by having the children perform role-plays. Look at different possible responses and outcomes. Ask the children to comment on the choices and outcomes.

{Section Two}

Your Feelings

Activity 8
How do I respond?

Objectives: To help children be more aware of how they respond to other people's emotions and the choices they make. To encourage children to make responses which are more beneficial to them and others, with healthier outcomes for all.

What you need
• Feelings Cards (If using this activity with younger children you may need to select some of the easier feeling words such as Happy, Sad and Angry.)

What to do
• Ask the children, "Why is it important to know when someone else is sad, angry or feeling another way?"

Possible answers: So we can respond in an appropriate way. Perhaps we would choose to move away from them if they are angry and we feel scared or maybe we would comfort them if they were sad and needed our support

Work through the following examples to further explore this topic.

Example One
• Show the children the "Sad" feeling card.
• Discuss why the dog is feeling sad – perhaps he is lost or hungry. Ask the children to think of other words that mean the same as sad – such as unhappy, miserable.
• Ask, "If someone is sad, how might you feel? How could you respond? What would you do?" Possible Answer: Ask them if they want to be alone or would rather talk.
• Discuss possible outcomes for each suggestion. Ask, "Would this be okay or would it possibly make the situation worse?"

Example Two

- Show the children the "Angry" feeling card.
- Discuss why the man is feeling angry. Ask the children to think of other words that mean the same as angry.

- Ask, "If someone is angry, how might you feel? How could you respond? What would you do?"
  Possible answers: "Move away, ask them what's the matter, tell them to calm down."

- Discuss possible outcomes for each suggestion. Ask, "Would this be okay or would it possibly make the situation worse?"

- Continue with other examples if appropriate.

Optional Activity

Worksheet: How Do I Respond — Help the children to complete the chart on the next page.

HOW DO I RESPOND?

Draw pictures or write descriptions about how you might respond to other people's feelings in the chart below.

Other Person's Feeling	How might I feel?	How might I respond?	What might happen next?
Sad			
Angry			
Excited			
Scared			

Activity 9
Short Stories and Role Plays

Objective: To help children be aware of their own and other people's feelings in response to various life situations.

What you need

- Feelings Cards
- A short story relating to FEELINGS will need to be selected for this activity. This activity can be repeated again with other selected short stories. Alternatively, the class or group of children can make up their own short stories.

What to do

- STEP ONE
  - Read a short story to the children. Pause the story when there is a relevant question to ask about how the people or characters might be feeling. (Pause points for questions and discussion are marked with an * in the sample story below.)
  - A child could be asked to select a feeling card that best describes how that person/character is feeling and why. This discussion on feelings could be extended during or after the story telling to include when the children may have felt this way?

Sample short story: Johnny bought some candy before school. * He was just about to put some in his mouth when a group of older kids came along and demanded that he hand the candy over to them. * They threatened to get him after school if he refused. * Johnny handed over the candy. * He then ran away and found a corner by himself and cried. *

- STEP TWO
  - Introduce the idea that most of the time we have a variety of choices as to how we could respond to challenging situations. We may get stuck in patterns that are not very helpful to ourselves or others.
  - In the short story that has just been read, discuss the variety of responses and possible outcomes that could give the story a different ending.
  - If using the sample story provided, introduce the idea that Johnny has some other choices as to how he could respond to the older kids.
  - Discuss the possible responses and outcomes using the choices below as a guide.

Choice 1: Say, "No" and run away. Possible outcome?

Choice 2: Hand over the candy to the bullies. Possible outcome?

Choice 3: Tell a teacher. Possible outcome?

Other choices you decide. Possible outcomes for each one?

Extension Idea

Choose a short story which involves feelings and win/lose situations. Tell the story then choose a small group of children to role-play all or part of it.

Ask the children to act it out again, only this time say 'freeze' at each point where the main characters have a choice of a particular response or reaction. Discuss possible options for each character at this point. Ask children to choose which responses would create win/win situations.

Ask the children to make up and act out a new version of the role play using the responses which they feel would create a win/win outcome for everyone.

As a group, you may like to record the possible options of win/win responses as a reminder for Classroom and Playground behavior.

Activity 10
Newspaper Articles

Objectives: To help children to develop more awareness of their own and other people's feelings.
To explore feelings and their impact by creating newspaper articles.

What you need
- Feelings Cards
- Writing Books
- Computer (Optional)

What to do
- In pairs or on their own. Ask children to pick three feelings cards (at random) and create a newspaper article/story based on these feelings.

- Have the children record in a daily journal all the good things that have happened to them or others in the school or local area. A computer can be used for this if available as it is easier to cut and paste later.

- At the end of the week the children pick one or two situations and write a short story for the class newspaper. e.g.. Jamie won the under 9's freestyle in the swimming carnival last week. He felt very excited and proud that he had won.

- Ask the children to illustrate their story.

Activity 11
create a story

Objective: To generate interest in and awareness of feelings through story telling.

What you need
• Feelings Cards
• Pen and paper to record their feeling words

What to do
• In small groups of three or four: Ask the children to pick a card each and write down the feeling word they chose.

• Ask the children to replace the cards before passing the full set to the next group.

• The next group can then shuffle the pack and chose their own cards.

• Repeat this process for each group.

• Then ask each group to make up a short story, role-play or a song using their chosen feeling words.

• Ask the children to perform their story, role-play or song.

• The other groups can act as an audience and may like to try to guess the feeling words that are being acted out.

Activity 12
Find the Missing Word

Objectives: To help raise children's awareness of feelings which come to the surface in a variety of situations.
To teach children a range of feeling words and how to express and communicate them verbally.

What you need

- Feelings Cards
- Worksheet: Find the Missing Feeling Word
- A Soft ball to throw around the circle.

Preparation

- Photocopy reproducible worksheet. Cut out the individual sentences and paste them to some colored cardboard.

What to do

- Arrange the cards with the sentences that you made up from the worksheet face down on the floor or table.

- Ask children to sit in a circle around the cards.

- Say "We are going to throw the ball to each other and whoever gets the ball can pick up a card. Read it to yourself first, without showing it to anyone else, and see if you can guess the missing feeling word. Then read the sentence out loud, using your choice of feeling word."

- Throw the ball to a child and begin the activity.

- Ask other children to identify which word is the feeling word in the sentence.

- If the child who catches the ball can't think of a word ask them to read out the sentence and say 'blank' when they get to the feeling word. The other children can be asked to volunteer appropriate words. There may be more than one word which is okay for each sentence.

- Repeat this activity, allowing other children to have a turn.

- Continue with this activity until you run out of sentences or until the energy level drops.

Extension Ideas

Ask the children to create their own sentences with a missing feeling word in it, then pair up and try to guess each other's feeling word. Swap with other children in the group. The missing words could be mimed to add more fun to this activity.

The children could also create a whole story of their own with missing feeling words in it. They then make a jumbled list of the missing feelings words at the end of their story. The children can exchange stories and fill in the missing feeling words.

Optional Activity

You could then have them do role plays for a number of the situations from the worksheet.

Find the Missing Feeling Word

Think of situations when you have the following feelings. Write in the boxes below to describe these situations.

I feel .... when my big brother pushes me around.	I feel .... when my little sister tells on me to a parent.
My mom was .... when I accidentally knocked over and broke her favorite vase.	My dad was .... when my 14 year old sister ran away from home.
Jason was .... when he found out he was going on vacation with his family.	My dad had a busy day and when he got home he felt ....
It was raining and Sally couldn't think of anything to do, she was	Laron felt .... when some of the other kids said nasty things to him.
Cindy felt .... when she fell over and cut her knee.	The little kitten was very .... when I found her in a tree.
When my pet dog died I felt very	Zac felt .... because it was his birthday tomorrow.

Activity 13
Create a Game

Objectives: To encourage children to have fun as they learn more about feelings by creating their own board games.
To encourage older children to interact with and support younger children.

What you need

- Feelings Cards
- Materials to construct board games

What to do

- In small groups of three or four: Ask the older children to design a board game to help teach younger children about feelings.

- Board game ideas could include: Play as teams. Move to a square, pick a feeling and mime the feeling, or make up a sentence omitting the feeling word. If the player's team guesses in 30 seconds, the player moves to next square and plays again.

- You could provide copies of the Feeling Cards to use in the game or have the children design their own set.

- Allow the groups to construct their board game. This may be done over a number of days.

- The groups could then take their completed games to a younger class in the school and play it with the younger children.

{Section Three}

Using sound, Movement and Music

Activity 14
Using Sounds

Objective: To help children explore, express and release a range of feelings, using sound.

Cautionary Note: It may be difficult to use this activity in certain situations, such as in a school classroom where it may disturb others who are in close proximity. It may bring to the surface feelings which need further processing. Extra support from a qualified counselor may be appropriate in some cases.

What you need
- Feelings Cards

Preparation
- Go through the set of feelings card and remove those that are difficult to express using sound, e.g. adventurous, creative, responsible.

What to do
- Ask a child to pick a card at random from the pack and to hold it up and tell the others what the feeling is. Ask them all to express the feeling using sound, e.g. SAD – wail, cry, HAPPY – laugh, SCARED – scream, whimper.

- Continue choosing different cards until the energy level drops.

Other options for expressing feelings using sound:

• Go to the beach where there is no one around and scream.

• Scream into a cushion or pillow.

• Cry or wail until you don't want to anymore.

• Laugh until you run out of laughter.

• Watch a funny movie and laugh out loud.

Extension Idea
The Power of Laughter

• Ask the children to stand in a big circle.

• Ask the children to move towards the centre of the circle while making the prolonged sound "Ae - ae - aeeeee" and waving their arms in the air. The group bursts into laughter as they meet in the center.

• After the first bout of laughter, ask the children to move back to the starting position and repeat the process saying "Oo - oo - oooo".

• For the third and fourth times make the "Eh- ehh" and "Oh - oh" sounds.

• Discuss The Power of Laughter and how it can help us to change how we are feeling. (Note for teachers — Laughter actually increases the level of serotonin in the body, Serotonin is a chemical which helps to maintain a "happy feeling" and seems to help with healthy sleep patterns, calming anxiety, and relieving depression.)

• Discuss with the children how they can create more laughter in their lives, such as watching a funny movie, telling jokes, playing fun games with friends.

Optional Activity

Worksheet: Sounds and Feelings — Ask the children to complete the worksheet choosing feelings and linking sounds to these.

sounds and Feelings

Pick four feelings and write one in each section. List any sounds that can be used to express these feelings.

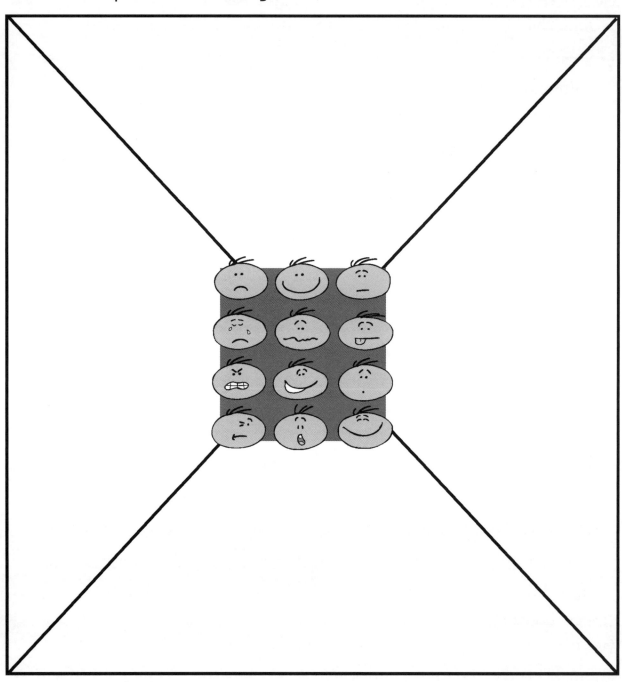

Activity 15
Using Movement

Objective: To help children explore, express and release a range of feelings, using movement.

Cautionary Note: It may be difficult to use this activity in certain situations, such as in a school classroom where it may disturb others who are in close proximity. It may bring to the surface feelings which need further processing. Extra support from a qualified counselor may be appropriate in some cases.

What you need
• Feelings Cards

Preparation
• You will need to go through the set of feelings cards and remove those that are difficult to express using movement, e.g. adventurous, responsible.

What to do
• Ask a child to pick a card at random from the pack and to hold it up and tell others what the feeling is. Ask them to express the feeling using movement and body language/expression not sound i.e. mime the feeling, e.g. SAD — walk in a sad way, hang head, drooped posture, sad face, HAPPY — smile, dance, SCARED — scared face, hands over face, backing off in terror.

- Encourage children to walk around and feel the feeling and express it with movement.

- Continue until the energy level drops.

Discuss

Ask the children "How can we tell how someone is feeling by their body language, movement and facial expression?"

Extension Ideas

- 'Feeling Freezer' Activity - PLACE the feeling cards — Angry, Sad, Scared and Bored — in the four corners of the room. Have the children walk around the room in a circle. Call out one of the feelings. The children have to rush to that corner and freeze in a pose expressing that feeling. Last child there or any that are moving sit out until the next round. Continue until one child remains.

- SAY to the children, "Let's see how easy it is to change our emotional state from feeling unpleasant to pleasant." Choose one of the unpleasant feelings and ask the children to close their eyes and think of a time when they felt this feeling deeply. Ask them to feel the feeling within their bodies and shape their body to the feeling. Have them express the feeling through movement. Now ask them to think of a fun time — Have them switch their feeling, stance and movement. Discuss how easily we can change our emotional state by focusing on positive thoughts. Try it with other unpleasant feelings, such as stressed and anxious to calm and relaxed. Have them feel the emotion of anger and then try to smile and say something in an angry way. Discuss the results.

Optional Activity

Reproducible Worksheets: Body Reactions A & B — Provide the children with a copy of (for younger children use Body Reactions B). This helps to reinforce how our body reacts to different emotions.

Body Reactions A

Our bodies react differently to different emotions. We show emotions through our facial expressions, muscle tenseness, volume of our voices and even how we stand. Cut the words and pictures below and glue them into the matching feeling.

ANGRY	SAD
SCARED	**WORRIED**

crying	clenched fists	crying	clenched fists
shaking	butterfiles in stomach	shaking	butterfiles in stomach

Body Reactions B

Our bodies react differently to different emotions. We show emotions through our facial expressions, muscle tenseness, volume of our voices and even how we stand. Write body reactions or draw pictures to match the feelings below.

ANGRY	SAD
SCARED	WORRIED

Activity 16
Combining Movement and Sound

Objective: To help children to be aware of the feelings inside their body, and to allow the expression of these feelings, using movement and sound.

Note: Movement and Sound are powerful ways of bringing feelings to the surface and to release locked up feelings.

Cautionary Note: It may be difficult to use this activity in certain situations, such as in a school classroom where it may disturb others who are in close proximity. It may bring to the surface feelings which need further processing. Extra support from a qualified counselor may be appropriate in some cases.

What you need
• Feelings Cards

What to do
• Ask the children to sit in a circle.

• Ask them to brainstorm a list of feelings, and write them up on a board where everyone can see them. Try to have each person come up with at least one or two feelings. You can use the Feeling Cards instead if you wish and get participants to choose 1 or 2 cards.
(With younger children use the Feeling Cards have them choose a feeling and an animal that they could pretend to be to express this feeling, such as an angry lion, or a sad dog, or an anxious rabbit. Ask them to express the movement and sound this animal would make.)

• Next, have the participants choose 3 feelings that they often experience in their life, and write them down or talk about them, saying how they affect them.

- Out of these three feelings, ask them to choose the one which has the most effect on them and their emotional state or behavior.

- Ask them to come out to the center of the circle, one by one, to express their chosen feeling with a movement and a sound and then to freeze their body in one position. All members of the group are encouraged to come into the centre of the circle, but should not be forced. Please respect the right of individuals who choose not to participate. Continue until all participants are in the center in their frozen poses.

- On the count of three, ask everyone in the center to do their movement and sound altogether as a group. A range of feelings may be expressed from happy to sad or angry.

You may be amazed at how powerful this expression is. For some people this exercise may bring up a lot of anguish and pain from deeply buried feelings.

- Now ask each member to come to the front of the group to watch while the others in the group repeat the expression of feelings together using sound and movement.

- When the exercise is complete, it is very important to allow each person to debrief, and to express how he or she is feeling. Further support may be needed for some children who have brought powerful feelings up to be released.

As mentioned previously this may bring up strong emotions so you will need to be prepared, as a group leader to deal with these. Some participants may need extra support and counseling, to deal with their emotional pain.

This exercise is designed to encourage the expression of emotions, and to help to release them from the person's body. Often we have layers of buried emotions, and movement and sound are powerful ways to help set the energy in motion of the emotion! More than one session may be needed, to assist with release of these emotions. It is healthier to have the emotions cleared and released than to keep them stored in the body for years.

Activity 17
Using Musical Instruments

Objective: To explore and express a range of feelings using music and sound.

Warning Note: It may be difficult to use this activity in certain situations, such as in a school classroom where it may disturb others who are in close proximity.

What you need
- Feelings Cards
- A variety of musical instruments or other items that create sound

What to do
- Ask the children to sit in a circle.

- Place the instruments in the middle of the circle.

- Have individual children choose a feeling card. Let them choose an instrument that they feel will best represent this feeling and play a rhythm or melody. The other children can then guess the feeling.

- Choose another individual and repeat the process.

- Children can also work in groups with a variety of instruments and one feeling card. Give them time to create a song based on their group's feeling card. Each group then presents their song to the class.

- Discuss the effect of music and sound on our emotions. Discuss how it can lift up us or bring us down. Ask the children for examples from their lives.

{Section Four}

Pleasant and Unpleasant Feelings

Activity 18
Pleasant and Unpleasant Feelings

Objective: To help children to be aware of and explore a range of pleasant and unpleasant feelings.

What you need
• Feelings Cards
• White Board and marker or Blank Sheet of Paper if unavailable

Preparation
On the Whiteboard or the Paper, write two headings:
• Pleasant Feelings or Feelings that help us feel good.
• Unpleasant Feelings or Feelings that don't make us feel all that great.

You may like to select a number of easier feeling words for younger children.

What to do
• Introduce this session with a short explanation and discussion. Adapt the language to suit a particular age group.

• Say to the children "Today we are going to explore our feelings. We all experience a range of feelings every day as we react to situations and other people in our life. Some of these feelings help us to feel good inside while others don't make us feel all that great."

(It would be helpful here to provide a few examples, such as bullying, teasing, holidays, birthdays, or ask the children to think of situations where they feel good or not so good.)

- Next, say to the children, 'I have some cards with feeling words on them and I am going to hold them up one at a time and ask you whether you think this is a feeling that helps you feel good (pleasant feelings) or not so good (unpleasant Feelings)."

- Using the set of feelings cards, hold one card up at a time and ask the children which heading it should go under, pleasant or unpleasant feelings? Using a dry erase marker write the feeling word under the correct heading.

Note: some of the feelings cards are neither strongly pleasant nor strongly unpleasant, you may like to create a third heading for these cards and call it neutral feelings.

Discussion/Explanation

Explain that it is natural to experience all of these feelings. It's okay to feel all the emotions, the trick is not to hang on to the unpleasant ones and let them affect you. You can communicate and express these feelings in non-violent ways without blaming others. Discuss ideas to help do this, such as Journal Writing, Drawing, Dance, Movement or Talking it over with someone.

Explain that you become powerless when you blame others because you are not taking responsibility for your part. Explain that it is important for your emotional health that you let go of these feelings and move on.

Note: Ways of exploring and expressing a range of emotions are covered in the next four activities.

Activity 19
Exploring Unpleasant Feelings with Movement

Objectives: To raise the children's awareness of the effects of unpleasant feelings on their own and other people's bodies.
To help them recognize and respond to others people's unpleasant feelings.

What you need

- Feelings Cards
- White Board and marker

What to do
Warm up Game - Feeling Freezer

- Place the following Feelings Cards — Angry, Sad, Scared and Bored - in the four corners of the room. (If you only have the set of small feeling cards, you may like to write the feeling words on a large piece of paper so they are easily visible.) Show the children where they are.

- Ask the children to walk slowly around in a circle. Explain to them that you will call out one of the feelings and they are to rush to the corner and freeze in a pose expressing that feeling. You may need to model this to them first. The last child there or any who are moving are asked to sit out. Continue this activity until one child remains.

- Stop at the end of each freeze pose and ask the children how they know when someone is feeling like this - Discuss their posture, body and facial expression, e.g. Angry - fists clenched, face wrinkled up.

Recognizing signals from our body

- Continuing on from the previous game, draw the following grid on the whiteboard with only the feeling word and have the children help you to fill in the possible body reactions section.

Feeling	Possible warning signals and body reactions
Anger	Red face, clenched fists, loud voice, aggressive posture
Sad	Drooped shoulders, crying, head down, lump in throat, loss of appetite
Scared	Paralyzed, want to run, shallow breathing, shaking, tense muscles
Worried	Knot in stomach, butterflies, tense muscles, trembling.

- Ask children for each feeling "How do we know when we or others are feeling this way?"

- Now we have explored a range of unpleasant feelings, the next activity will help children to find ways of expressing them using a range of creative expression ideas.

Activity 20
Expressing Unpleasant Feelings with Journaling and Art

Objective: To help children express unpleasant feelings using creative expression, such as art, letter or journal writing.

What you need
- Feelings Cards – larger ones or make a larger heading on paper
- Paints
- Writing paper
- A journal
- Drawing paper

Note: A journal can be made using an inexpensive exercise book. Children can design their own cover for this book using a sheet of art paper.

What to do
- Ask the children to think of a situation in their life, which brought up an unpleasant feeling like anger, sadness or hurt. Discuss if appropriate.

Choose one of the following activities to help them to explore and express this feeling or explain all of them and let the children choose which one they would like to do.

Letter Writing

• Ask the children to write a letter to explore this negative feeling. They could write a letter to someone to tell them how they feel or just pretend they are writing to a Help Page in a magazine. The purpose of this activity is not to send the letter but just to allow the expression of the unpleasant feelings. The letter can be torn up later, if appropriate.

Journal Writing

• Ask the children to write in a Journal about this situation and describe how they felt. Stimulus questions may be useful. "What happened? How did you feel? How did you act? How might the other person have felt? How did they act?"

Art Expression

• Ask the children to draw and paint a picture to express their unpleasant feelings. They could be encouraged to use colors and shapes to represent this feeling or they could just create their own picture.

Discussion

This could be followed by a discussion if children wish to share their letter, journal or artwork.

Extension Idea

Let the children use a computer for letter writing or journal writing. Programs such as Powerpoint can be a powerful tool to express feelings where they can incorporate images and sounds.

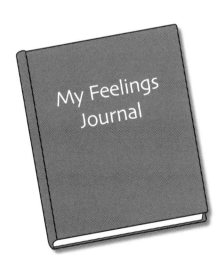

My Feelings Journal

Activity 21
Exploring Pleasant Feelings

Objective: To raise the children's awareness of the effects of pleasant feelings on their own and other people's bodies.
To help them recognize and respond to other people's pleasant feelings.

What you need
- Feelings Cards – larger ones or make a larger heading on paper
- White Board and marker

What to do
Warm up Game – Feeling Freezer

- Place the following Feelings Cards or your own Flash Cards – Happy, Relaxed, Caring and Excited – in the four corners of the room. Show the children the cards.

- Ask them to walk slowly around in a circle. Explain to them that you will call out one of the feelings and they are to rush to the corner and freeze in a pose expressing that feeling. You may need to model this to them first. The last child there or any who are moving are asked to sit out. Continue this activity until one child remains.

- Stop at the end of each freeze pose and ask the children how they know when someone else is feeling like this from their posture, body and facial expression, e.g. Happy – smile, dance pose.

Recognizing happiness in our body

• Following the previous game, draw the following grid on the whiteboard with only the feeling word and have the children help you to fill in the possible body reactions section.

Feeling   Possible body expressions and reactions

Feeling	Possible body expressions and reactions
Happy	Smiling, light-hearted happy voice, open friendly posture
Relaxed	Lowered shoulders, laying or sitting down, relaxed muscles
Caring	Warm expression, open welcoming posture, head tilted
Excited	Butterflies, tingling muscles, energetic vibrant posture, wide eyes

• Ask for each feeling "How do we know when we or others are feeling this way?"
• Now we have explored a range of pleasant feelings, the next activity will help children find ways of expressing them using a range of creative ideas.

Discussion

Discuss generally how we can help ourselves to feel more pleasant feelings. More activities on how to change mindset from unpleasant to pleasant will be offered in the next section.

Activity 22
Expressing Pleasant Feelings with Journaling and Art

Objective: To help the children express pleasant feelings using art, letter or journal writing.

What you need
- Feelings Cards – larger ones or make a larger heading on paper
- Paints
- Writing paper
- A journal
- Drawing paper

Note: A journal can be made using a notebook. Children can design their own cover for this book using a sheet of art paper.

What to do
- Ask the children to think of a situation in their life, which brought a pleasant feeling like happiness, caring or excitement. Discuss if appropriate.

Choose one of the following activities to help them to explore and express this feeling or explain all of them and let the children choose which one they would like to do.

Letter Writing

- Ask the children to write a letter to explore this pleasant feeling. They could write a letter to someone to tell them how they feel. They could create a thank you card to someone who helps them to feel happy.

Journal Writing

- Ask the children to write in a Journal about this situation and describe how they felt. Stimulus questions may be useful. "What happened? How did you feel? How did you act? How might the other person have felt? How did they act?"

Art Expression

- Ask the children to draw and paint a picture to express their pleasant feelings. They could be encouraged to use colors and shapes to represent this feeling or they could just create their own picture.

Discussion

This could be followed by a discussion if children wish to share their letter, journal or artwork.

Extension Idea

Let the children use a computer for letter writing or journal writing. Programs such as Powerpoint can be a powerful tool to express feelings as they can incorporate images and sounds.

{Section Five}

Changing the Emotions

Activity 23
Change the Feeling

Objective: To show the children how to change their mindset and thus to change their feeling state.

Note: This exercise is purely to encourage a more positive, beneficial state of mind. This does not negate the concept that some feelings such as sadness and anger need to be processed and expressed.

What you need
- Feelings Cards
- A selection of music (optional) to evoke a range of feelings such as happy, sad, angry
- Bell (optional)

What to do
- Select a number of feelings cards such as Excited, Happy, Sad, Angry, Calm, Relaxed, Worried, Joyful.
- Explain to the children we are going to have some fun changing how we are feeling.
- Ask the children to smile and to try to mime an angry body posture and move in an angry way at the same time. You will probably find that the children break out in laughter because this is difficult if not impossible to do.

- Show the children your selection of cards. Say, "Now we are going to have some more fun. In a moment I would like you to think of a time when you were sad (hold up the sad card) and then to express this using your body posture, movement and facial expression."

- Then say, "Change to happy. (You could use a bell or other musical note here.) I would like you to think about being happy and act it out using your body posture, movement and facial expression."

- Music can be used for this activity and you can still use verbal prompts during this activity if appropriate.

- Repeat this activity with other cards such as excited calm, angry, relaxed, worried joyful.

Discussion
Discuss the fact that there are lots of ways to change your emotions to a more pleasant one. What are some of these? Work in pairs and come up with a list. When children have finished write combined ideas on the board or a large piece of paper. This list may include: Listen to music, Dance, Sing, Watch a funny movie, Exercise/walk/run, Talk to a friend.

Activity 24
Creating More Pleasant Feelings

Objective: To help children explore pleasant emotions and how to experience them more often.
To create a poster to encourage this.

What you need

- Feelings Cards — larger ones or make a larger heading on paper
- Paints
- Writing paper
- Drawing paper

What to do

- Discuss with children when are times when we feel good? "How can we feel good more often?" Be aware of when you are feeling angry or sad wanting to change or stay there?

- Ask the children to choose 3 feelings from the set of cards you would like to have more often. "How can you create them?" Brainstorm and list possible answers, such play with a friend, write in journal, dance or sing.

- Use these answers to help create a Poster for the home or classroom to remind everyone that we can feel good more often, such as Our Happy Classroom or Our Caring Home.

- Allow the children to work individually or in groups, to list ideas, plan the layout and illustrations then draft their poster.

- Encourage the children to illustrate the poster to make it look inviting to read regularly.

- Place them somewhere in the room where everyone can see them. These posters can be used to remind the children that we can choose to have positive feelings more often.

Be Happy

Play with a friend.

Talk to someone.

Write in your journal.

Sing and dance a happy song.

Smile!

Extension Idea

Encourage children often when you notice them expressing positive actions towards others. Have the children to write down the names of other children they have seen being positive throughout the day and place it in a colored box. The names can be checked at the end of the day and recognition given.

Activity 25
Creating a Feeling Affirmation Card

Objective: To help children to create their own special feeling message or affirmation card.

This can be used daily to help reinforce positive affirmations to themselves.

What you need
- Feelings Cards
- Art Materials

Preparation
- Paints and card or drawing paper cut into card size.

What to do
- Design, draw and color a border around a whitecard or drawing paper. Ideas: dolphins, sports themes, flowers, rainbows, butterflies, animals or just shapes.

- Encourage the children to use feeling words.

- Write a special sentence or few words to help you feel good. (This could be typed out on the computer and cut out to fit inside the border of the card. e.g. Magic happens when you are caring, Happiness Helps, I am Loving.)

> **Swim with the dolphins**
> **Fly with the birds**
> **Be true to your friends**
> **Let your dreams be heard**

Extension Idea

The children could make a framed affirmation card by following these directions.

What you need

Strong, thick cardboard · Craft Glue · Scissors · Art Resources
Computer · Colored paper · Plastic knife · Pencil Ruler

What to do

Cut out 2 pieces of cardboard frame size. Take one of these pieces (call one piece A and the other piece B) and using a plastic knife cut a rectangle in the middle of piece B (which will be the frame). The smaller piece of cardboard cut out of piece B will become the support at the back (piece C).

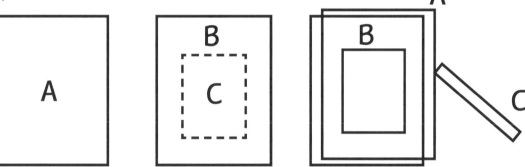

Paint all three pieces of cardboard on one side only with a thick layer of white paint.

Have the children draw and paint a design on piece B with the rectangle cut out of the middle (the frame).

The children can also paint the white side of the other 2 pieces of cardboard, A and C, with colors or a design.

The children now choose an affirmation e.g. 'I am happy and joyful', to go on colored paper in the centre of the frame, piece B. Using a computer, type and print the affirmation on colored paper and cut it out so that it fits inside the frame. Place the affirmation onto the non-painted side of the frame so that the writing is centered and shows inside the painted frame. Place the non-painted side of piece A to the non-painted side of piece B, (the frame). Then use the support piece C onto the back of piece B so that the whole frame stands up, similar to a photo frame.

Activity 26
Creating an Appreciation Card

Objective: To help children show appreciation and caring for someone in their life.

What you need
• Art Materials

Preparation
• Paints and card or drawing paper cut into frame size.

What to do
• Choose, create and give a card to someone else to show appreciation.

• Design draw and color a border around a white card or drawing paper. Ideas: dolphins, sports themes, flowers, rainbows, butterflies, animals or just shapes.

• Ask the children to write a special message of appreciation on the card, such as "Thank you for listening to me, Thank you for sharing." Have children share these with someone who is special.

Adventurous

Excited

Lazy

Relaxed

Creative

Beautiful

Embarrassed

Caring

Grateful

Calm

Playful

Angry

Loving

Free

Tired

Hurt

©YouthLight, Inc.

©YouthLight, Inc.

©YouthLight, Inc.

©YouthLight, Inc.

Sad

Fun Loving

Joyful

Bored

Scared

©YouthLight, Inc.

Happy

©YouthLight, Inc.

Responsible

©YouthLight, Inc.

Upset

©YouthLight, Inc.

Disappointed

©YouthLight, Inc.

Surprised

©YouthLight, Inc.

Wonderful

©YouthLight, Inc.

Worried

©YouthLight, Inc.

In the Home

The Activities and Feelings Cards can be used by parents to help their children explore and express their feelings.

They also support the development of more effective communication and social skills.

You can use them to help children feel more in charge of their own feelings and to help them develop a resiliency to other people's negative attitude.

The Activities and Cards can be used in a variety of situations that may arise on a daily basis such as friendships, bullying, 'put-downs', teasing and others.

The activities have been divided into five sections, as described. This allows you to easily locate an appropriate activity to suit your needs.

• "My Feelings" – Helps children to explore and express their own feelings

• "Your feelings" – Helps children to become more aware of other people's feelings

• "Using Sound, Movement and Music" – Helps children to express and release their feelings

• "Pleasant and Unpleasant Feelings" – Helps children to further understand the effects of different kinds of feelings.

• "Changing the Emotional State" – Helps children to change their emotional state and increase the presence of more positive emotions to improve their health and well-being.